# My State
# NEVADA

By Christina Earley



TABLE OF CONTENTS



A Crabtree Seedlings Book

Crabtree Publishing
crabtreebooks.com

# School-to-Home Support for Caregivers and Teachers

This book helps children grow by letting them practice reading. Here are a few guiding questions to help the reader build his or her comprehension skills. Possible answers appear in red.

## Before Reading:

- What do I know about Nevada?
  - *I know that Nevada is a state.*
  - *I know that Nevada has hot, dry summers.*
- What do I want to learn about Nevada?
  - *I want to learn which famous people were born in Nevada.*
  - *I want to learn what the state flag looks like.*

## During Reading:

- What have I learned so far?
  - *I have learned that Carson City is the state capital of Nevada.*
  - *I have learned that the Hoover Dam supplies power to Nevada, Arizona, and California.*
- I wonder why...
  - *I wonder why the state flower is the big sagebrush.*
  - *I wonder why there are so many neon lights in Reno.*

## After Reading:

- What did I learn about Nevada?
  - *I have learned that you can ride roller coasters in Las Vegas.*
  - *I have learned that the state animal is the desert bighorn sheep.*
- Read the book again and look for the glossary words.
  - *I see the word **capital** on page 6, and the word **canyon** on page 15. The other glossary words are found on pages 22 and 23.*

# NEVADA

I live in Reno. The **neon** lights are very bright.

The Truckee River runs through my city.

Nevada is in the western United States. The **capital** is Carson City.

Fun Fact: Las Vegas is the largest city in Nevada.

The state animal is the **desert** bighorn sheep.

The big **sagebrush** is the state flower.

We grow a lot of hay in Nevada. Some of it is used in horse stables.

Fun Fact: Nevada grows 286,000 tons (259,000 metric tons) of hay each year.

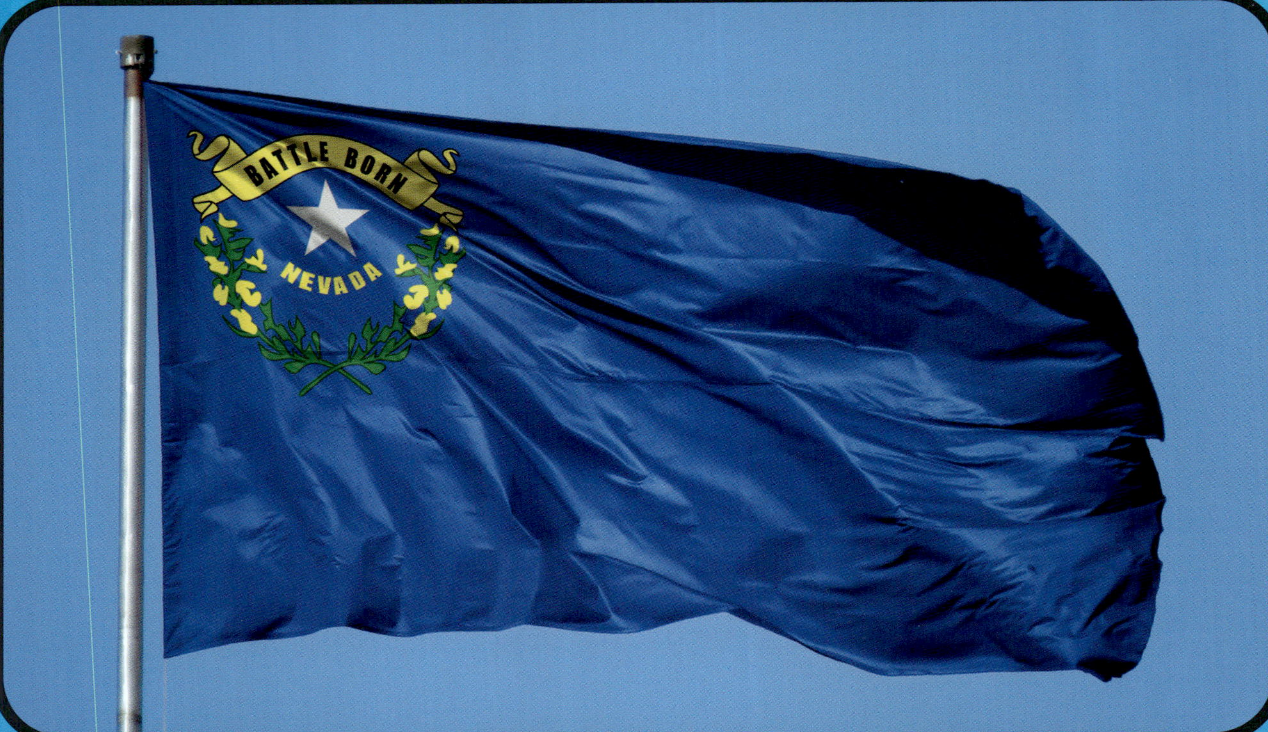


My state flag is blue. It has an **emblem** with a star and a wreath in the upper left corner.

My family likes to watch the Vegas Golden Knights play hockey.

I like to visit the Hoover Dam. It is in the Black **Canyon** of the Colorado River.

Fun Fact: The Hoover Dam supplies power to Nevada, Arizona, and California.

My family goes boating on Lake Tahoe.

I like to ride the roller coasters in Las Vegas.

Actress Jaylen Barron was born in Nevada. Baseball player Kris Bryant was also born in Nevada.

Fun Fact: Former First Lady Pat Nixon was born in Ely, Nevada.

My family and I go backpacking at Great Basin National Park.

I enjoy biking in Black Rock Desert.

# Glossary

**canyon** (can-yin): A deep valley with steep sides, often with a stream or river running through it

**capital** (cap-ih-tuhl): The city or town where the government of a country, state, or province is located

**desert** (deh-zert): An area usually covered in sand or rocks, where there is very little rain or water

**emblem** (em-blum): A picture or design that represents an idea

**neon** (nee-on): Bright and colorful

**sagebrush** (sayj-brush): A type of shrub with a strong smell that grows in dry areas

# Index



# About the Author

Christina Earley lives in sunny South Florida with her husband and son. She enjoys traveling around the United States and learning about different historical places. Her hobbies include hiking, yoga, and baking.


Written by: Christina Earley
Designed and Illustrated by: Bobbie Houser
Series Development: James Earley
Proofreader: Melissa Boyce
Educational Consultant: Marie Lemke M.Ed.

Photographs:
Newscom: Joel Marklund/ZUMA Press: p. 13; Joe Robbins/ Icon Sportswire 573: p. 18 right
Shutterstock: VarnaK: cover; Kit Leong: p. 3; Joseph Sohm: p. 4, 23; Don Mammoser: p. 5;Volina: p. 6, 22; Sean Pavone: p. 7, 14-15, 22; Jen DeVos: p. 8, 22; Brendan Bucy: p. 9, 23; VICTOR TORRES: p. 10-11; Konstantin Tronin: p. 11; Millenius: p. 12, 23; superjoseph: p. 15; IM_photo: p. 16; ZikG: p. 17; Eugene Powers: p. 18 left; Arlene Waller: p. 20; Elizabeth A.Cummings: p. 21
whitehouse.gov: p. 19

## Crabtree Publishing

**crabtreebooks.com 800-387-7650**





Printed in the U.S.A./072023/CG20230214

**Published in Canada**
**Crabtree Publishing**
616 Welland Avenue
St. Catharines, Ontario
L2M 5V6

**Published in the United States**
**Crabtree Publishing**
347 Fifth Avenue
Suite 1402-145
New York, New York, 10016

**Library and Archives Canada Cataloguing in Publication**
Available at Library and Archives Canada

**Library of Congress Cataloging-in-Publication Data**
Available at the Library of Congress

Hardcover: 978-1-0398-0525-5
Paperback: 978-1-0398-0557-6
Ebook (pdf): 978-1-0398-0621-4
Epub: 978-1-0398-0589-7